I don't feel like writing
says the author

I don't feel like writing says the author

Jasmin Hajro

Appearantly authors are people too…

What to share anymore…
after 45 books….

It's Sunday 15 november 2020,
the corona crisis is still happening…
In the Netherlands
we're in a partial lockdown…

I woke up late...at 14:00 hours
yesterday I went out selling,
I sold 1 set of greetingcards for christmas
to a regular customer of my business,
and I sold 2 pens to another regular customers..
They buy every year…
thank god…

After that I wanted to get something done….
But my old laptop did't cooperate…
fuck...what annoying that was….

Eventually I made a Free author website…
It will be online forever…
you can find it at
www.jasminhajro6.webnode.nl

I give away 10 books on it…
my whole first series of books in one boxset (bundle)
(they're in english)
So you can go check it out and grab a free copy…

I would like to write a bestseller…
evrytime I finish a book…
there'se the thought….the hope...this could be the one…

and then...nothing happens...

Then...what do I do ?

I start writing my next book.....

Did you get it ?

The secret.....

I hate to work in the yard and mow the lawn...
but I do it evrytime....

Did you get it ?

The secret.....

In times when I'm tired,
it's raining...
I don't feel like doing it...
don't want to go to work...
don't want to go out selling door to door
but I still do it....

I get ready and go out selling....

Did you get it ?

The secret....

If you didn't get .....reread the past 2 pages.....

The future is looking good financially...
I am selling an average of 500 greetingcards a month...
so I earn about 500,- euros a month...
I need about a 1000,- euros a month to independantly earn my
living....I am halfway there....

By now more than 500 books of mine are sold…
including free and paid titles….

I am still living with my mother….
Whan I was a cook, I earned about 1000 to 1200 euros a month…
and focused on creating a fortune
by saving and investing in the mutual funds
stocks and bonds on the stock market…

so Going out of the house to live on my own wasn't my priority…

In 2011 I got some severe problems with my mind…
because of the braindamage that I have…
lost that cooking job…
and after that…
couldn't reach that level of income again…
untill summer last year…
but I left that summerjob…
and went on selling greetingcards for my 2nd business…
that I still do…
I am doing that for more than 5 years…
(a few months in the summer last year, I had a job on the side)

I failed at my first business..
and because I didn't reach minimum income level
in the past 8 years…
bills and debts piled up….

But good things are gonna happen…
1 you are reading a book of mine, yeey
2 Kobo will pay out 30 euros in royalties next week
3 I will receive 650 euros every month for the next 1,5 year from
the government, to help me succeed as a business owner
4 It seems I will get some money back from the IRS

A fool and his money ?

Maybe…
You know …if you go around telling about your money…
bad peple will come to get it from you…

But they came in 2013 or in 2014
when I had pennies
when I had nothing…

They also came in 2018 or 2019…
gave me herione in my fingertips…

And they'll probably come again in the future….

So should I just shut the hell up about money
about my earnings
about my sales and customers
and my business revenu….

???

Maybe it's embarresing to to tell that I only earn 500 euros a
month….

But as you probably have noticed…
I am raw…
my writings are raw…
because I am real…
I talk from experience and reality…

and in life and reality ….shit happens…
people fail….people do bad things…
progess is slow…
and so on…

But good things are going to happen….financially…
like I told you before….

Amd I am halfway there

to being completely successfull
as a salesman
as a business owner
and as a entrepreneur and writer…

Hooray….

In the past 5 years of being in business I had to learn
persistence…
perseverence…
to ask for help…
to save money...even when I have little…
to be generous...even when I have little…
and to keep on writing and keep on working ...no matter what…
and
to focus on the coreactivities…
doing only the things that produce results…
the result of earnings and profits..
or the potential of earnings and profits…
(like with writing another book, that may sell and earn me some
money)

and also to study my profession
of selling…

it helps….

I work by myself…
You learn to do most things yourself…
when you start a business and don't have the funding to hire
people….
I have some people that will deliver my flyers,
when I order flyers…
but they work on commission...
So I also don't have a team of 10 or 50 people
give a free copy of my book…
to get some reviews in return…
I write

selfpublish
translate …
and share and promote my books by myself…

I work about 6 days a week and spend the 7th with my sister and
her kinds….
Except for those weeks...when I take more rest…
sometimes I also work on the 7th day…

That's how I get more done…

To save myself the time and effort…
my last book and this book
I am writing in english
from the start
to save time on having to translate it…

How about that productivity hack ??

This is actually a boxset (a bundle of 3 books in 1)
and the first one that you're reading right now…
is a good one for writers and authors….
Don't you think….

Did you get the Secrets ?
To being productive anyway…
to getting a task done anyway…
to get your ass to work and start working anyway…

when you don't feel like doing it…

What is the title of this book ?
How did I feel about writing ?
But what did I do anyway ?

That's the secret of productivity & succes in reality…

I watched and listened to some vidoes on youtube from Lee
Milteer…..and you should do the same…

A dollar for 7 pages ?

If you think that….
you're missing the point and the secrets…

that will make you more productive and make you more money…

Read it again…

This booklet is for my dearest mother
mama azema
because of her support
I have had the time to write a lot of books and build my business..

Thank you

In this book you'll discover the

story of the financial expert from Bosnia &
his writings...
for readers, salespeople, business people,
writers, fortune seekers and
lovers of true stories...

&

whitepaper Through the crisis

&

book Overcoming tough times

<u>The bio of author Jasmin Hajro, nice to meet you</u>

Hello dear reader, how are you ?
Thank you for buying my book.

My name is Jasmin Hajro,
I was born on July 6, 1985 in Bosnia.
As refugees, we came to the Netherlands 21 years ago.
After having completed school & worked at several jobs ...

On 17 December 2012, I founded my first company:
investment firm Jasko.
After a successful first year, I unfortunately had to close that
company. After a short period of rest, unemployment and
temporary work. I started again as an entrepreneur.

On September 1, 2015, I founded establishment Hajro.

(We say establishment instead of company,
because we do a bit more than just sell stuff.
Like providing jobs,
donating to 40 different charities,
and helping people to live richer.)

Since the beginning the core activity is,
selling sets of greeting cards, door to door.
Nowadays the product range has been expanded.

With, among other things, the selling of my 40+ books.

The royalties of my books are donated to the charity:
foundation Giveth Life.
From there more than 40 other charities receive donations.
And by buying this book you support more than 40 charities.
Thank you.

My company is now Hajro bv
and has stocks.

For more information about my company
& the foundation,
go to my website : **www.hajro.eu**

Who the hell is Jasmin Hajro ?

Well that is me, in the pictures ...left & right at the top of my website

at the right side side I am holding my first bundle of books.

I was very happy, proud and tired as you can see at my pale face...

At the top left is my logo (it's also the logo of my business, establishment Hajro)

But this website is about writing, writings and books, ebooks, printbooks,

audiobooks and

even videobooks.

For booklovers

& for people who don't like to read ...Get it ?

Don't like to read ??

Buy an audiobook or videobook, click play, sit back , relax

and enjoy....

I've read somewhere what an author page should include,

like : an extensive biography, summary of work, emailadres

for fans to connect

and so on....

Because I have many responsabilities, I will include those things
step by step. So come back once in a while
to check out the new stuff and updates.

Okey , my name is Jasmin Hajro
I am blessed to be 34 years old,
I live in Doetinchem, that's a city in the Netherlands...
I was born in Bosnia Hercegovina, we lived in a village called Gora,
I started going to school , played around like kids do ,
untill the war started...

We then moved a couple of times within Bosnia
and eventually fled the country to the Netherlands.
In the Netherlands we lived several months in different
asylum centres for refugees in different cities..
Eventually we got a house in Doetinchem..
I went to school and learned the Dutch language...

I did about 1 year of karate...
In my teens I loved playing videogames,
then we played it on the Nintendo...long time ago...
I also learned chess and was interested in that...
At school I was good in languages,
but now I hardly remember any of the French that we
learned...
My father eventually also came to the Netherlands,
before that it was just Mama, me and my little sister..

But after a while my parents divorced

and my father moved away to another city, where he had some relatives.
He remarried and I went to live with my father for about a year,
being in puberty and not on my best behavior....
It didn't work out, so I moved back to Mama and my sister..
I started some experimenting with alcohol and the funny stuff...
Hanging around with the wrong crowd , getting a bit into trouble...
Eventually after I almost killed myself by taking too much drugs...
I left everything behind...

Started living healthy, reading, got an empty book to write in,
so I wrote in my journal,
started working, took the jobs I could get,
played chess, studied chess, went to a chess club,
became a bit of a hermit because I didn't want to spend my time
with those guys from the oldtimes...

I worked as a carwasher,
worked as a cleaner,
worked as a deliverer of mail and marketing and newspapers,
worked in kitchens
as a dishwasher and also prepared dishes...
The longest time an an employee was at Landal greenparks,
started as a dishwasher,
became a cook, worked there 4,5 years.

In that time got very interested in finance (money matters)

saving and investing..
I read a lot about it,
took a couple home study courses,
got experience by investing my own money...
Eventually in 2012 I started my first company
investment firm Jasko...
I invested my own money and that from my 5 clients..

I did pay out the 10% return that I promised..
Unfortunately it wasn't profitable enough to make a living,
so I had to close it.
My mama calls me Jasko, it's like my nickname...
(that's why the company was called Jasko)

I did have a few girlfriends, the relationships didn't last
long...

I started my 2nd company on 1 september 2015,
establishment Hajro, that sells greetingcards and giftmugs
door to door
and donates part of it's profits to 40 charities in the
Netherlands.

It has been a challenge,
been thru a lot B.S.
stuff happens they say..
a lot sh*t happened, I talk more about that in my video :
Challenges in having your own business, in real life..

We do keep our promise (our USP) as a establishment,
meaning that we have people working and pay them,
and that we did donate more than 600,- euros to

those 40 charities that we support
and that we do help people to live richer
with our Savings newsletter and free ebook : Build your
Fortune...
Untill now we have found about 1000 customers in city
Doetinchem
and town Didam.

I changed my approach...
to a flexible approach or flexible attitude...
Asked for help, applied for all kinds of arrangements
and took a job parttime...

I also wrote about that in my newest book :
Meer succes met een flexibele instelling
(More success with a flexibele attitude/approach)

Well the the flexible approach works,
because I earned 1313,- euros in july 2019,
more than what I averaged in the months of the past 6
years...
It has been a struggle....I am the first to admit that..

But I keep up the spirit...

Establishment Hajro will become a Private company...
the legal form with which you can sell stocks of your own
company...
I am very excited about that ...

I will also probably shift to position of being an energy
advisor...
and do that next to the selling of greetingcars, giftmugs and

books...

What about a subsidiary Hajro Author Coaching ,
to help starting authors to write their book
and get their books out there &
in front of people with our little newspaper...?
I already have our own little tiny newspaper...
Called Jouw Krant (Your Newspaper)
Who knows...

By now I have made the shift,
monday 12 august 2019
I start working as an energy advisor....
I am very very excited about that...

My mama became my first customer,
I arranged for the switch to a better energy supplier,
at 23:43 hours.
Well if it's good enough for Mama
en our home, it's good enough for you
and your home.

By december 3rd my company Hajro
became a Private company...
I fully committed to it
and designed Unique greetingcards
the website is www.hajro.eu
and I will be an entrepreneur
and write more books
untill retirement....

I am now writing in my 11th journal...

a few years ago I started making books
out of my life experiences, my knowledge
my skills and my experiences as a business owner
and as a salesman and also as an author...
It took me a bit encouragment...
but eventually I also jotted down my lifestory in books
and share it with the world...
(My lifestory is in my Victory books, as you now)

Thanks to some great people and their selfpublishing
companies...
my books are available in 190 countries worldwide
in different stores.
27 of my books are in Dutch
and I have translated 11 into English
actually 12 into English, the 12th became an videobook...

It will take me some time to translate all my titles into
English
and produce the audiobook and videobook editions
but You have plenty to read and enjoy allready
with the first translated 12 books.

I have earned a bit more than 400,- euros in royalties by now,
most of that I earned with the Kobo Plus (their subscription
service)
and I have donated more than half of that to
those 40 charities that we also support with establishment
Hajro...

Don't worry, we always prove our donations
by publishing banking statements on our Blog...

We are open and honest....thinking that is the best way to go
to build good relationships with our customers.

Some of my books are free as an introduction or promotion,
you might want to start with those
if this is the first time that you stumble upon me and my
writings..

If you have read some of my books and are a customer
I am very happy with you..
that I found a fan...
I have resolved to make every new book
better than the last one
so that I keep you happy
and then I am happy too.

More will be added...
for now Thank you for visiting
I hope you love my books..

Enjoy them
and please be so kind to tell your bookloving friends and
relatives
about me and my books.
Huge thanks.

My goal is to help 100 million people all around the world
with my books
If that adds up to about 100 million euros,
it will be 50 million euros for those 40 charities that we
donate to.

You are free to help out.

Like in the painting below...
my books with their gold, silver and bronze covers
read and enjoyed by people
all over the world

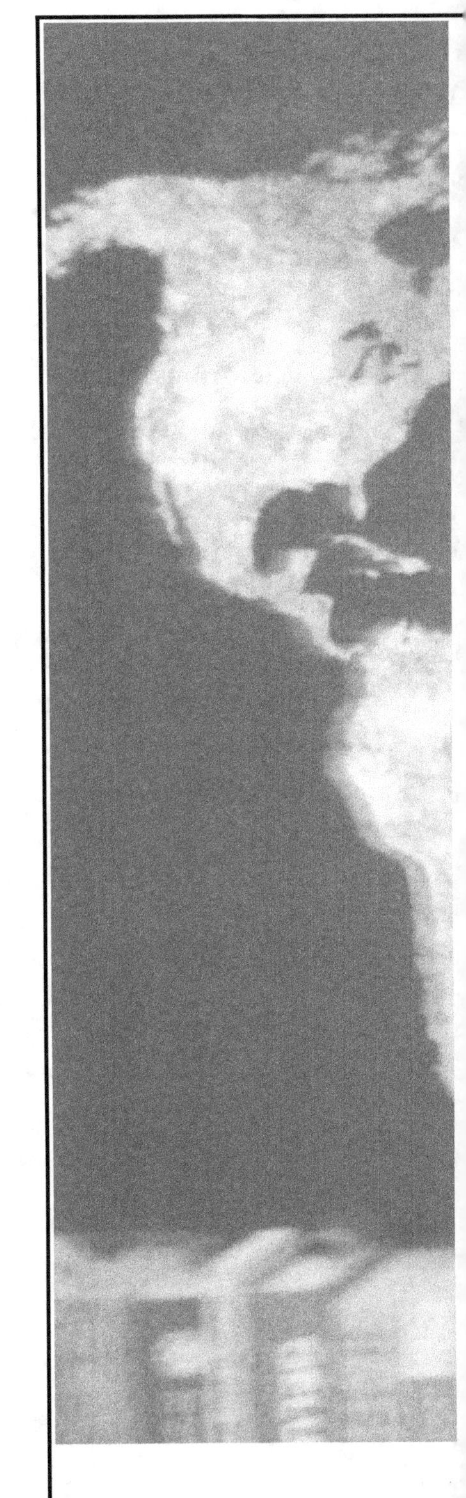

My work :

Victorious series :

-
-
-
-
-
-
-
-

Work to shine series :

-
-
-
-
-
-
-
-

-
-

mama Azema series :

-

You legend series :

-

-

Legacy series :

-

-
-
-
-
-
-

Bundles (boxsets) of my books & my other titles

-

-
-
-
-

-
-
-
-
-
-
-
-
-
-
-
-
-
- View more

Future projects...

-

Never miss a next new release of mine....

Get an automatic update message

in your email

Whenever I release a new book or translation..

Sign up with a click at :

https://books2read.com/author/jasmin-hajro/subscribe

Why should I listen to this guy ?

Jasmin is
honest and tells you how it was,
how it is , what worked and what didn't..
See video Challenges in
having your own business, in real life
Jasmin has experience with saving,
investing and money building and made himself
 a good financial expert
with years of study and experience.
Watch video Your Money Expo part I & part II
Jasmin has experience in sales, still selling door to door.
Jasmin has obviously experience in running a business or 2 .
Maybe 3...
If you consider my books a business...
Why ?
It requires products (books, ebooks, audiobooks, videobooks)

promotion & marketing (making people aware of what I have to offer)
and selling, asking people politely to buy
and customers...
and someone to do the work..(in this case that means me, working my a*s off)
Just like a business.

Jasmin works most of the time and is happy most of the time
 (For you to figure out the link between those 2)

"If you want to keep your customers, you'd better be honest and treat them good"
Jasmin is also
writing for more than 10 years,
A strategist
and consultant
and a comedy lover
plus he loves to help people; see the donations and free ebooks.
(excuse his spelling mistake, here and there)

 What's in it for me ??

First of all ...by buying from Jasmin you also donate to 40 charities...
2nd...His books will help you to enjoy exciting true stories, to improve your sales ...even double them...

to make more profits, to write your book or series of books,
to get a grip on your money and make it grow
and also Jasmin will help you to reduce stress and live
happier.....
Strategies and stuff that works for you

What more is in it for me ?

My books will help you to build a good retirement
Help you to overcome addictions & change your habits
Help you see that your situation isn't a disaster & make you laugh
And help you overcome your tough times & difficulties
Encourage you to persist in achieving your goals & dreams.
I donate part of my royalties to charity.

Here'se a list of some stores where my books,
audiobooks, videobooks, ebooks and even our unique greetingcards
are available...

Shop in your favorite store, for my books as Paperbacks,
Ebooks, Audiobooks, or even as Videobooks,
and you can also order a set of unique birthday greetingcards

that I designed & also some author Merchandise from me...
(at Gumroad)

Just click on the link of your favourite store :

Kobo , Amazon , Barnes & Noble , Apple books

Mijnmanagementboek.nl , Streetlib store ,
Bookdepository

Payhip (discounted ebooks)

Walmart

Notion press store (in India) , Buecher.de (in Germany) ,
24symbols

Scribd , Pothi (in India) , Flipkart , Selz

Don't like to read ?
Get an audiobook or videobook,
sit back... relax....click play...and learn and enjoy..
For my audiobooks, videobooks and other recordings go to :
Patreon

Leanpub
(at Leanpub, you donate directly to some international

charity, by buying a book of mine, like Collective Scholarships & Oxfam america)

Books 2 read

(at books2read, click on the book and the buy button, and you will see it available at different stores, libraries and also subscription services like Scribd)

Smashwords

(At smashwords more than 126 people got a free copy of one of my books)

Bol.com , Weltbild , Baja Libros , Thalia

Internet Bookshop Italia , XinXii

At Angus & Robertson , in Australia

Lulu , in the United States of America
(for paperbacks & ebooks visit the Hajro store at Lulu)

Fishpond , also in Australia

Chapters Indigo , in Canada

Exclusive books, in Africa

Goodreads

Plenty of stores and plenty of books available for You...

For free previews, free ebooks, a personal letter and to keep in touch with me, signup for free below.

Give me a chance to keep in touch with you..

I will write more books and I want to share them with you

Subscribers get a free bundle of books..

For the Jasmin Hajro newsletter...

click here and signup for free (opens in new window)

or use the signup below

If you are curious about my financial expertise,
watch the video's below
in wich I explain everything to you

Weird facts...

#1. I am 34 years old and I still live with my mother
(Things just worked out a bit different)

#2. I never use a hairdryer
(Just can't stand the noise of it)

#3. I jog a couple of times a week and I smoke tabacco..

#4. I drink a litre coffee a day or more

#5. I sometimes go to sleep with my clothes on.

____

If you like my work and want to support your author & my
future projects....
You can make a donation or leave me a tip ,
using paypal with the Donate button below.
Thank you generously

Donate

Me with my selfdesigned greetingcards
the unique ones that we sell at establishment Hajro

Jasmin Hajro
SECRETS OF WRITING AND
SELLING BOOKS

Jasmin Hajro

Secrets of writing and selling books
If you think that from just reading this book your life will
change... Don't bother to read it... If you understand that you get
results from taking action on what you learn... and you are a
starting author or just have a book or 2 fi
€15,99 PAPERBACK
BUY NOW

Jasmin Hajro

Challenges in having your own business, in real life

**HOW TO OVERCOME TOUGH TIMES &
DIFFICULTIES**

JASMIN HAJRO

Jasmin Hajro

how to Overcome tough times & difficulties
The book that I did not want to write. Including painful moments
and tough times. But I did it anyway, and it helps you to
relativize & overcome your tough times. Piece from the book:
Aging sucks It sucks, right? Every year, you become a year old
€14,99 PAPERBACK
ORDER NOW

HOW TO GROW YOUR MONEY & BUILD A GOOD RETIREMENT IN 2 HOURS PER MONTH,

FOR MOMS, DADS, CAREER WOMEN AND BUSY PEOPLE

JASMIN HAJRO

Jasmin Hajro

how to Grow your money & Build a good retirement in 2

hours per month,
how to Grow your money & build a good retirement in 2 hours
per month, for moms, dads, career women and busy people..
Gives you all the steps you need to take, every month and every
year. To make the money that you save, grow faster. The returns
€24,99 PAPERBACK
ORDER NOW

the Ultimate Winning Strategy
for entrepreneurs & salespeople
+ Double your profits, extended

Jasmin Hajro

"the number one reason for success
in business is high sales"
-Brian Tracy-

Jasmin Hajro

The Ultimate Winning Strategy, for entrepreneurs &

salespeople

Discover & implement : - the Ultimate Winning Strategy for entrepreneurs - Your advantage over your competition - 2 Real life examples that show to you that the Ultimate Winning Strategy for entrepreneurs, is proven and works - As bonus a number of

€29,99 PAPERBACK

ORDER NOW

TRIUMPH

Jasmin Hajro

Triumph

These 6 most read & bestselling books of mine, I have bundled together for you in 1 convenient bundle. They are book Victory the exciting true story about growing up in Bosnia untill the war started, then moving a couple of times because the enemies came

€24,99 PAPERBACK

ORDER NOW

VICTORY

AN EXCITING TRUE STORY

JASMIN HAJRO

Jasmin Hajro

Victory

Victory, part 1 The first part of my autobiography. I take you to my native Bosnia. Where I was born and lived. Until the war started. Then we moved a number of times, and finally fled to the Netherlands. You also receive a Bonus book

€14,99 PAPERBACK

<u>ORDER NOW</u>

Jasmin Hajro

Triumph 2

In this 2nd bundle of books you'll get all my other titles which I have translated into English, so people worldwide can enjoy my work and improve their lives: The bio of author Jasmin Hajro & book Victory II the sequel to the exciting life story & book R

€24,99 PAPERBACK

ORDER NOW

JASMIN HAJRO

Victory 2

Jasmin Hajro

Victory 2

Victory II the second part of my autobiography When I started to smoke, drink and take other rubbish. When I survived a coma. When I collapsed and stopped drinking. When I worked myself up from dishwasher to cook. Plus a free bonus boo

€14,99 PAPERBACK

<u>ORDER</u>

Be a buddy

and introduce me to your bookloving friends and relatives,

by sharing this website with them

use the social media share buttons below..

I'll give you a free ebook for it...

Thanks anyway..

Share

Thanks a lot buddy,

for your Free ebook & more...

<u>just click here</u>

Thanks for visiting...

Come back soon...

Kind regards,

Jasmin Hajro

Through the crisis

(referring to the Corona crisis

what I did to get through it)

What is a life without diligence ?

– Ludwig van Beethoven -

In january 2020, I sold 121 sets of greetingcards,
and 10 pens.

I received 10,- euros in bookroyalties

It adds up to E 625,50 euros

In february 2020
I sold 69 sets of greetingcards and 8 pens..

I received E 2,63 euros in bookroyalties

Total E 358,13 euros

In march 2020
I have sold 70 sets of greetingcards

and 2 pens.

I received E 1,18 euros from booksales.

Total E 353,18

And I received E 1000,- from the government

In april 2020

I have sold 77 sets of greetingcards
and 20 pens.
I received E 0,60 from booksales

Total E 405,60

And I received E 1000,- from the government

In may 2020
I have sold 92 sets of greetingcards

and 25 pens

I received E 20,- because of some islamic festival

Total E 505,-

I have written and published

books and whitepapers

They dutch titles are :

Je kan het

Wat het beste werkt ? Na 7 jaar ondernemen

Word miljonair in sales

Victorie 4

Voor Saartje

Gewoon doorgaan

Meer succes met verkopen & ondernemen

Wil je meer succes met huis aan huis verkopen ?

Hajro Franchise

Work to shine serie, boek 1 t/m 10

Legacy serie, boek 1 t/m 10

Het geheim van afvallen, het geheim van goed leven &

mijn schrijfsels.

Voor mijn fans

De geheimen van goede sex, 30 boeken schrijven, een
levenspartner vinden & geld verdienen zittend op je reet.

The english titles are :

Secrets of writing and selling books

Challenges in having your own business, in real life

Our neighbour died,

he had a lung issue for years.

It was a weird time,
it still is a bit…

We're wearing face masks in the train.

But most businesses , the library and so on
are all open again….

I sell greetingcards and I write books,
we also sell my books
that's my work

You might say…
that I kept myself busy
all the time
all the months
that this ''crisis'' was
and is going on

What else was I to do ?

It seemed the best way..to get through it
To keep myself busy

I hope you and your family got through it well
I hope you are safe

Thanks for reading my short whitepaper,

on the following pages

you can read one of my books

that will help you get through

all kinds of times

Happy reading

<u>book Overcoming tough times</u>

What are tough times?
Isn't that different for everyone?

Perhaps something like tiring times.

Times that make you tired.

I worked in a tapas restaurant in Arnhem,
called Ramblas.
The food was delicious,
but I waanted to do something else,
then work in the dishes and the kitchen.

I started a home study for Wft basic Advisor,
when I worked in that restaurant.
In the evening at home I heard that my uncle Ibro,
who lives in Bosnia, had died.

Things were finally going the right way.
I finally had work and earned money,
could pay my bills.
And reduce my debts.

Well then thas bad news came.

It was as if all energy went out of me.

I have very happy memories of
my childhood in Bosnia.

My family is part of my happy memories.

Someone once asked me what I was missing?
Because I had almost no contact with my uncle.

Apparently, those things go like that,
contacts & connections fade ....
Especially if you live far away from each other.

What I missed was his humor,
it always feels good and joyous when I was there.
And going to Bosnia on vacation is no longer
the same, because the people you go for
no longer exist.

I have thought about it...
Because I have already written 11 books.
The one you are reading now is the first part of my new series:
Work to shine.

What kind of book would be good for many people?
What kind of book would be helpful to many people?

What should be in it, what would it have to give to readers?

Even if it is only recognition,
periods I went through &
that they are going through.
That they can relate to.
To know that you can get through anything.
No matter how painful it is
and no matter how bad it seems, at the moment.

Or comfort.

Maybe relativation,
to attenuate their troubles and their situation &
see them in the right perspective.
They're just like a threshold on the road,
that you really will get over.

To be honest, I do not want to write this book.
I do not feel like writing it.
I really had to force myself ,
to sit down &
start writing.

It is Sunday for God's sake.

July 1st
A new month started,
it is beautiful sunny weather outside.

I got up before noon, for once.

Yeah, for some miraculous reasons,
I am almost 33 years old and I still struggle
to get up in the morning on time.

So what does this Workaholic do?
On such a nice Sunday?

Starting on a new book series &
writing a book that he actually does not want to write.

Well if you've read my book Victory,
then you know that one time in Bosnia

when I was a little boy
I had to sit nude in front of the house. As a punishment.

Because of those kind of fokking things,
I did not really want to write this book.

Anyway,
I have already started ....

So what's in it for you, to know what kind of
extreme punishment I received?

Well, whatever is bothering you,
no matter what kind of tough time you're going through now.
Ans no matter how difficult it may be for you ...

You will never have to sit naked in front of your house,
as a punishment.

You see,
your situation is not that bad.

(That is relativizing, that is to say
relativation or taking the edge off it)

Perhaps there is a better translation ?

But you know what I meant, right ?

Let's go back to Uncle Ibro for a moment,
he left behind a wife and two daughters.

I'm just very sorry that I did not do something for him,
when it was still possible.

I live in a country where I have much more possibilities,
then they have in Bosnia.

I would have liked to send him money every month
And have visited them every year,
or a number of times a year.
Sent them gifts and spent more time with them.

I would have liked him to get to know my great company
& to show him my 11 books which are for sale in 190 countries
worldwide...
And the good foundation that I founded.

But that is not possible anymore,
Uncle Ibro is deceased ....

<u>People of gold</u>

For me that was Grandpa Vejsil and Grandma Ziba.
They too lived in Bosnia.
Grandma and step grandpa actually.

Maybe because they have more experience with parenting,
then my parents.
Or because I never got a beating from them.

It was always great fun with grandpa and grandma.

<u>A lot thanks to her</u>

My father's oldest sister, Aunt Rahima.

Thanks to her, we were able to go to the Netherlands.

To get away from the war.

I owe a lot to her.

<u>In a short period of time</u>

In the period of time, that Uncle Ibro died,
I went to work
& then back home again.

I had enough of it
and I left.

In that period,
that lasted perhaps a half year or 1 year.

Aunt Rahima died of cancer,
Grandma Ziba died.

I went to Bosnia and there
I have carried her coffin for a while.

There was a long line of people and the coffin was passed on.
All the way to the grave.

We had a friend of my mother
in our neighborhood: called Ria.

She drank a little too much and had
a strange fear : she was afraid to walk up the stairs.

It was nice with her, when she came to visit.

She also died of cancer.

In that short period of time.

And then I heard that Grandpa Vejsil
also had died.

A while before, grandmother and grandmother had already split
up.

But still.

That was 5 people in a short period of time.

At that time we received many letters from collection agencies
and bailiffs.
Our bills that they doubled the amounts that we had to pay
and that was all according to the law.

Yah Yah.

They are legitimate thieves.

So I was very angry and sad then.

Very very angry. Warlike angry.

And sad.

As you understand,
I would have liked to have done something more for them.

Spent more time with them.
Have given them more.

And I would loved to show them,
how far I have come.

From being 1 night homeless,
to writing 11 books & publishing them in 190 countries
worldwide
Plus a good foundation &
a company with 16 subsidiaries.

But now it's too late for that.
They are dead.

I stopped using drugs,
after I had taken too much,

and ended up in a coma.

Well if you use yourself or know someone who does that ..
And if you see it as a waste of potential &
want to be clean
or help someone else to become it.

Then it might be good to know,
what I did afterwards.

That was just as important.

I decided, of course, not to do it anymore.
I could not do it anymore.
I think I got an anxiety attack,
when I tried to smoke a blunt.
Because I was shaking,
and wondered if I was going to get a heart attack.

What I did after ...

No more buying that stuff.
Stopped dealing with people who use it.
Yes, I was at home a lot and it was shitty,
but it was better.

I started to become more fanatic with my chess hobby
and kept myself busy with it.

I went for walks.

I thought of people who used as LOSERS

I once collapsed and fell to the ground,
and after that I stopped drinking

alcohol.

What I did after ...
Was not going to the pub anymore.
Didn't go out to clubs anymore.
Drank a lot of tea and coffee.

Went hiking.
I read.
Listened to audiobooks and watched motivational videos
on youtube.

I wrote.

I didn't go anymore to places and people
where alcohol was consumed.

Yes I was a lot of times at home, like a hermit.

But it was better.

<u>Bills and debts</u>

See bills and debts not like a burden,
but as responsibilities.

And people who still have to receive money from you,
are people who trusted you
or have faith in you.

And for that kind of people you are going to make things right.
No matter how much time it takes you.

Put all your bills in 1 folder and put that thing out of sight,
in a drawer or something.

Emplane some cash money around you in your house.

And focus on earning money,
stash money,
and take care of your responsibilities.

<u>Aging sucks</u>

It sucks, right?

Every year, you become a year older.

I thought so too.
And I especially disliked to become 30 years old.
Because I had heard or thought
that after your thirtieth year
you start to decline.
That everything is going to decay and won't function well.

And I thought about, when I become 80 years old,
and nothing functions anymore
to kill myself one way or another.

Until someone said:
The older you get the better it is

And that is the mighty fokking truth,
as far as aging is concerned.

Some children do not even become 10 years old.

Some people don't even become 18 years old.

But you are 30 or 40 or 50 years and having another birthday
& you can live for another year.

How a great gift is that ...
You can do and experience so much. And enjoy.
Be happy
The older you get, the better it is.

<u>The Better thing</u>

Failing and falling on your face is good for you.
And also is rejection.

Because then the Better thing comes on your path.

I had a solution for the banks,
neatly typed out and ready.
They did not want it.

A while after that,
out of my solution I made a book.
book the Lifebuoy for banks
" loyal banking "
(de Reddingsboei voor banken"loyaal bankieren")
The Better thing

I applied for a social wellfare for the 2nd time.
It was rejected.

I walked home,
and then wrote my 3rd book:
book Recipe for Happiness
the Better thing

That is how it will work out for you too.
Do not despair. Work towards your goals and dreams.
The Better thing is coming

<u>a Doing book</u>

Well, as you might already know in the meantime
I write short books.

And Non fiction.
Simply facts and life experiences.

With often things in them that you can do,
or must do.
Actions you can perform,
so that you get results.

You probably already understand that by just
thinking about 10 euros/dollars,
the 10 dollar will not manifest in your pocket.

But if you do something.
Like working for a while.
Then you will receive the 10 dollar.

I would love to recommend to you
my book Recipe for Happiness
(Also a Doing book)

It contains tips and advice that you can easily do &
that help you to have less stress.
To be happier and healthier.

And also help you a bit to overcome difficult times.

<u>Count on one hand</u>

That night on the street is actually the best thing
that has happened to me.

It has put pepper in my ass,
to go to work hard.
And to get more out of myself.

It has also taught me,
that very few people are always there for you.
You can count them on one hand.

Whatever you did,
and however you have behaved.
They are still there for you.

These rare few could be your mom and dad.

Thank them,
appreciate them.

Make some sunshine for them &

make them proud.

Well you now also know with which people you should
spend your time. And not with others.

<u>And that</u>

What I did after I stopped taking drugs and drinking alcohol
was also ...
Working

They were not always the nicest jobs.

But work has really changed my life.

That it will do for you too.

Work is your best friend,
you can always count on it.
You can always 'borrow' money from that friend
after you have worked.

Quote :" Work is the best therapy."
By Doctor Maxwell Maltz

So if you don't believe me, believe the doctor.

<u>Those meager months</u>

And what about those months when you only
earned a few bucks?

I will become a millionaire or die working towards it.

So about really fokking great.

My Victorious series of 10 books &
Another one,
show you:

That if you really want something,
then you can do it too.

No matter what & Whatever they say.

<u>That obvious recipe</u>

It goes something like this:

Write down what you want to achieve in life

Learn, Work & Persist until you realize it

About the same process as getting your driver's license.
Or cooking a meal.
Or getting your diploma.
Or writing a booklet.

Save a part of your money &
donate something to charities.

Keep reading, listening to audiobooks
and developing yourself. Keep growing.

Learn the 80/20 principle,
so that you will only do the most important things,
that give you the most results.

Then you will feel better about yourself &
that also helps you
get thru tough times.

<u>Learn that it does not matter what people say</u>

To achieve the things you want in your life,
the only thing that matters is : what you think and what you DO

If you experience this as a valuable book,
would you please be so kind

to recommend it
to the people that you know.

So that it helps them too with overcoming tough times.

Thank you.

<u>Extra page</u>

After failing with my first company.

I founded a new and better one.

After my burnout, that cost me 2 months of time

I picked myself up, and became active again.

I started working (selling), writing, jogging

and kept going again.

If I can recover & overcome, so can You.

You are designed tougher than

tough times.

I wish for you a lot of strenght &

the best things in life.

Kind regards,
Jasmin Hajro

P.S. If you want to share your experience with my book,
send me a little revieuw or email at
j.hajro@hotmail.com
Thanx.

<u>Small introduction with establishment Hajro</u>

Establishment Hajro is committed to helping the people
in the province of Gelderland,
by providing jobs and keeping people working,
by donating to more than 40 Charities,
and by helping people to live richer.

Today Hajro bv has it's own stocks
and a few subsidiaries.

We now have several products & services,
and we support more than 40 charities.

Visit us at **www.hajro.eu**
and discover what else we can do for you.

Hopefully you will become a raving fan & customer of us.

Kind regards,

Met vriendelijke groeten

Jasmin Hajro

Hajro BV

KvK 76564770

Unieke wenskaarten,
cadeaugeschenken & boeken :

www.hajro.eu

Author website :
www.jasminhajro.nl